ONCE UPON A BRIDE THERE WAS A FOREST

Kristen Palmer

BROADWAY PLAY PUBLISHING INC
224 E 62nd St, NY, NY 10065
www.broadwayplaypub.com
info@broadwayplaypub.com

Cover art by Will Lowry

First edition: July 2017
I S B N: 978-0-88145-724-7

Book design: Marie Donovan
Page make-up: Adobe InDesign
Typeface: Palatino

ONCE UPON A BRIDE THERE WAS A FOREST
was first produced by Flux Theatre Ensemble at the
4th Street Theater in New York, running from 6–20
December 2014. The cast and creative contributors
were:

EVERETT	Arthur Aulisi
BELLE	Becky Byers
JOSIE	Rachael Hip-Flores
MAN	Brian Silliman
WARREN	Chinaza Uche
EUGENIA	Kristen Vaughan

Director	Heather Cohn
Scenic design	Will Lowry
Lighting design	Kia Rogers
Sound design	Janie Bullard
Costume design	Stephanie Levin
Properties design	Sara Slagle
Stage manager	Jodi M Witherell
Assistant director	Sarah Amandes
Technical director	Claire Bacon
Master carpenter	Janio Marrero
Assistant lighting design	Asa Lipton
Master electrician	Ayumu Saegusa
Fight director	Adam Swiderski
Carpenter	Mike Mihm

The playwright would like to thank the following, Heather Cohn & Gus Schulenburg, Sol Crespo, Isaiah Tanenbaum, and all at FLUX Theater Ensemble who committed so beautifully to this play. All the actors who shared their voices and support during Tina's Wednesday classes; Mark Bly, Jimmy Maize, Daniel John Kelley, Lindsay Ferrentino, Rob Cardazone,and the Hunter College Theater Department. Michael Wright and the University of Tulsa. John and Rhoda Szymkowicz. Betty and David Michel; and always, Adam Szymkowicz

CHARACTERS & SETTING:

JOSIE, *female mid–late 20s.*
WARREN, *male mid–late 20s.*
MAN, *a presence of indeterminate age.*
EUGENIA, *female 40–60. Somewhat severe.*
EVERETT, *male 40–60. A dear papa.*
BELLE, *female early 20s. A sweetheart.*
MAGS, *a baby-bundle.*

An apartment in Brooklyn.
A dark wood.
A house in the country.
A soda counter.
A basement.
A wedding.

With infinite gratitude to Tina Howe.

This play is dedicated to my father.

ACT ONE

1.

(The sweetest of apartments. A bit cramped. A bit hemmed in. But the residents have made the best of it.)

(JOSIE wears an ironic apron and uses a feather duster.)

(WARREN reads The New York Times *while lounging in a little chair.)*

JOSIE: Do you think we should go away next weekend?

WARREN: Do you want to?

JOSIE: I think so. It's stifling here and I can't shake this cough.

WARREN: It's the overpass. I knew it before we rented the place but I still said yes.

JOSIE: It's a sweet place.

WARREN: It's poisoning you.

JOSIE: If it was poisoning me it would also be poisoning you so it's not so it's probably in my head so everything is probably fine.

WARREN: Are you sure?

JOSIE: I think so.

WARREN: Think or know?

JOSIE: Hard to say.

WARREN: It's probably fine.

JOSIE: Probably. So, what? A trip? A get-away? A stay here and explore weekend? What do you want to do?

WARREN: What do you want to do?

JOSIE: Oh—I could go—I could stay—

WARREN: I know what I want.

JOSIE: Warren.

WARREN: Come here.

JOSIE: I'm dusting.

WARREN: I see that. Come here.

JOSIE: What?

WARREN: I want to marry you.

JOSIE: Warren.

WARREN: What?

JOSIE: We've said.

WARREN: You've said.

JOSIE: But you agreed.

WARREN: I did not agree. I conceded. There is a difference.

JOSIE: You told me you understood.

WARREN: And I do. I do understand.

JOSIE: Then why bring it up?

WARREN: Because I want to. I want to marry you. I want to put a ring on your finger and wait for you at the end of an aisle and see you emerge all white dressed and flowered and I want to dance with you while our family and friends watch us and I want to love you for ever and ever until we're old and we bicker and we smell and our apartment deteriorates around us and we fall asleep with a kiss and grow cold in the bed and everyone agrees that we had the best ever love because we died together.

JOSIE: Oh—

WARREN: You will?

JOSIE: Oh Warren—

WARREN: Exactly. You must.

(WARREN *gets up and hugs and kisses* JOSIE *and twirls her around.*)

JOSIE: But—

WARREN: But what?

JOSIE: But—

WARREN: Finish your thought—

JOSIE: Before we tie the knot I need to take care of some things.

WARREN: Of course. A dress. Your mother. Your sister. A guest list. My parents. Rings. We need rings. First off. I should have had one already—that's the classy way to do it.

JOSIE: I wasn't going to say—

WARREN: You care though. A disappointment already.

JOSIE: No. It's fine.

WARREN: It's not fine. I'll have one on your finger in a fortnight.

JOSIE: A fortnight?

WARREN: Too long?

JOSIE: Just right.

WARREN: It is?

JOSIE: I'll be back by then.

WARREN: Back?

JOSIE: I want to at least try.

WARREN: Try what?

JOSIE: To find him. If I can find him before we put on the rings—that would be perfect. We'd have his blessing. He'd know. He could come for the wedding. He could walk me down the aisle.

WARREN: Josie—

JOSIE: He can give me away. He can shake your hand. You've never met. That seems wrong. He should meet you. That's the way to start.

WARREN: Don't do this—

JOSIE: I have to—I have to make it real—

WARREN: What's not real? I am real—

JOSIE: I know but—

WARREN: You're here, your life is here. Your work, me—

JOSIE: But, if he could see it, if I could just tell him—

WARREN: Josie—

JOSIE: He'll want to know about this.

WARREN: Of course he would but—

JOSIE: I need to find him. I feel it. Now I have a purpose. A reason. Warren. Really, it's the most important reason of all. It's us. It's our marriage. The start of a life. He'll have a son-in-law.

WARREN: Grandchildren.

JOSIE: Children?

WARREN: One—two—

JOSIE: One thing at a time.

WARREN: Okay—okay—but we don't have to wait.
We're lucky. We are so lucky. We can do whatever we
want. And I want to love you.

JOSIE: Oh—

WARREN: Don't you want that?

JOSIE: I do. I do! But I want to do it right, I want it to be
perfect. I want him to see me all grown up and happy.
That's something. In most cultures that's everything.

WARREN: I don't want you to go.

JOSIE: Just two weeks. If I can't find him by then. I'll be
back.

WARREN: Two weeks?

JOSIE: A fortnight.

WARREN: When you come back I'll have the ring. The
ring will have chip in it with a G P S beacon cause I
want to always know where you are.

JOSIE: I'll call every night.

WARREN: I don't want you disappointed.

JOSIE: It'll be fast.

WARREN: Okay.

JOSIE: I'll leave tonight.

WARREN: Tomorrow.

JOSIE: First light.

WARREN: You should stay.

JOSIE: I have to go.

WARREN: You don't. You don't have to go. You could
just say yes. Say yes. And come to bed and in the
morning we'll start planning together for the what's
next—

JOSIE: Warren—

WARREN: I just think. It's best to leave it, leave him. You have a life now. Your very own life—and you have me—

JOSIE: I'll be gone for two weeks. Only two. Just, call it a head-clearing—a heart-clearing—before the notion of wedding takes over. Before the ever after starts. Okay?

WARREN: I can come with you.

JOSIE: No.

WARREN: Why not?

JOSIE: It's better if I do this alone.

WARREN: No it's not.

JOSIE: It is.

WARREN: I am a good help.

JOSIE: You've got to get the ring.

WARREN: So?

JOSIE: You've got to make the plans.

WARREN: Not all the plans.

JOSIE: This one thing alone, and then, forever and forever everything else we'll do together.

WARREN: I like that.

JOSIE: Me too.

(*First light of dawn comes blinking through the window.*)

WARREN: First light.

JOSIE: Time to go—

WARREN: So soon?

JOSIE: I'll go west.

WARREN: Wait—just west? Can you be more specific?

JOSIE: A town on the other side of the mountains.

(JOSIE *drops her apron. Grabs a coat. Gathers her bags. Already packed*)

WARREN: Whoa—slow down.

JOSIE: We said first light.

WARREN: You need breakfast.

JOSIE: I'll pick some up.

WARREN: Let me make you coffee.

JOSIE: I'll get it on the road.

WARREN: You're taking the car?

JOSIE: Is that okay?

WARREN: Sure. Sure.

JOSIE: You understand.

WARREN: Sortof.

JOSIE: I'll be home in two weeks.

WARREN: Promise?

JOSIE: Of course.

WARREN: And you'll call every night?

JOSIE: I said I would.

WARREN: So you will.

JOSIE: Yes.

WARREN: And you'll be careful.

JOSIE: I'm not going to war.

WARREN: You know what I mean.

JOSIE: I do. I'll be fine. I'll call you at the first sign of a tear.

WARREN: At the first tightening of your throat.

JOSIE: At the first tremble of my heart.

WARREN: Let me come—

JOSIE: No. You stay. You build our love nest and I'll do what I need to do before I feather it.

WARREN: I love you.

JOSIE: I love you too.

(They kiss and embrace and JOSIE *exits.)*

2.

(A dark and stormy night)

(Lightning flash reveals a house on a hill.)

(A gate stands in the middle of the stage. A man in a heavy raincoat and a wide brim hat stands in attendance.)

*(*JOSIE *enters struggling against the wind and the rain.)*

JOSIE: Hey! Hey! Mister! My car broke down back along the road—

MAN: Triple A.

JOSIE: Excuse me.

MAN: Triple A. Call the triple A.

JOSIE: I don't have the triple A. My boyfriend and I— my fiancé and I don't drive out of town much so—

MAN: Short sighted.

JOSIE: Well—that's the way it is—is there a phone I could borrow? There's no reception here. And I am freezing. Could I go up to the house to get warm?

MAN: No.

JOSIE: Is there another place?

MAN: Not for miles.

JOSIE: Then, please? I just need the phone. Maybe dry off a bit—

MAN: The family has asked to never be disturbed.

JOSIE: I won't disturb them—I'll stay on the porch—

MAN: I don't recommend you go up.

JOSIE: So I can?

MAN: I don't recommend it.

JOSIE: Just to use the phone.

MAN: Things are never so simple.

JOSIE: It's freezing here.

MAN: Uh-huh.

JOSIE: And you just stand in this all night?

MAN: As is my job.

JOSIE: Then do something useful. Help me out.

MAN: You're sure to be disappointed.

JOSIE: Look. There's nowhere else to go. There's a house. I'd like to use their phone. I'm sure they won't mind.

MAN: Mmmm.

JOSIE: What?

MAN: They are expecting someone.

JOSIE: Who?

MAN: A nanny.

JOSIE: Tonight?

MAN: The baby cries.

JOSIE: All the time?

MAN: Ever since it was born.

JOSIE: I'm good with babies.

MAN: You are?

JOSIE: Oh yeah.

MAN: Are you the nanny?

JOSIE: Oh—yes. Yes I am.

MAN: Why didn't you say? Then go to the door. They will greet you and see how the baby takes to you.

JOSIE: Fine.

MAN: Good luck.

(The gate swings open and JOSIE *disappears into the storm.)*

(The MAN *remains at his post.)*

3.

*(*JOSIE *stands in the foyer of a lovely home. A delightful table with a bouquet of flowers, a chandelier over head, a deep red finely patterned carpet.)*

*(*MRS EUGENIA WRIGHT *and her daughter* BELLE *greet* JOSIE.*)*

EUGENIA: Don't stand dripping on the rug.

JOSIE: Sorry.

EUGENIA: No. No. It's fine. I just don't see why you're soaked. We sent a car didn't we?

BELLE: I thought we did.

JOSIE: I drove myself—

BELLE: You did?

JOSIE: Yes.

BELLE: See mother, young women drive all the time.

EUGENIA: Not now Belle.

JOSIE: The car broke down in the woods.

EUGENIA: And you walked?

JOSIE: One foot in front of the other.

BELLE: Up the hill?

JOSIE: I'm hoping I can use your phone—to fix the car.

BELLE: How would you use a phone to fix a car?

JOSIE: To call someone?

EUGENIA: Where did you say it was?

JOSIE: In the woods.

EUGENIA: Before the stream or after?

JOSIE: After, I guess, I don't remember fording a stream.

(EUGENIA *claps twice and the* MAN *from the gate appears.*)

MAN: Yes.

EUGENIA: Call a tow truck. A mechanic. Call the person who can deal with this poor girl's vehicle.

MAN: Of course.

JOSIE: It's fine. I can call—

EUGENIA: Nonsense. You need to get dried off, warmed up and then—well. We'll see if you can do anything about this baby.

JOSIE: I hear she's been crying?

EUGENIA: Ever since she was born.

JOSIE: Even when you hold her?

EUGENIA: When anyone holds her, when I hold her, when her father holds her, when Belle holds her, when Mr Livingstone holds her—

JOSIE: Mr Livingstone?

EUGENIA: The man.

JOSIE: Oh. Of course.

BELLE: She's horrible.

EUGENIA: Belle.

BELLE: Sorry.

EUGENIA: She is a baby and she is fussy. She didn't ask to be here. None of us asked to be here.

BELLE: But we adjust.

EUGENIA: Yes. We adjust. I think you should try immediately.

JOSIE: Try what?

EUGENIA: To calm her.

(EUGENIA *goes to open a little door. A terrific scream is released. She shuts the door.*)

JOSIE: That's a baby?

BELLE: That's her.

JOSIE: She never stops?

BELLE: When she eats. And one day last week.

JOSIE: Wow.

BELLE: We don't sleep anymore.

JOSIE: How old?

BELLE: Four months.

JOSIE: And your father?

BELLE: Oh—well. He's fine. He's got a gift of selective hearing.

JOSIE: I don't understand—

EUGENIA: Don't stand there gawking. Go in. Go in!

(JOSIE *does. The wails resume.* EUGENIA *and* BELLE *stand watching through the door.*)

(*The crying ceases.*)

EUGENIA: Oh my.

BELLE: It's quiet.

EUGENIA: How did you?

(JOSIE *comes through, carrying the babe.*)

JOSIE: I don't know—she's adorable.

BELLE: She really is.

EUGENIA: We couldn't see it before—she was so loud.

BELLE: We could give her a better name now.

EUGENIA: Margaret.

BELLE: I like that.

JOSIE: What was it before?

EUGENIA: Belter McGee.

BELLE: Screamface.

EUGENIA: Hollering Horror.

BELLE: Fat Mouth.

EUGENIA: Globber Blob.

JOSIE: Margaret's lovely.

EUGENIA: Well. The job is yours.

JOSIE: Oh—I—wasn't actually planning to be a—

EUGENIA: Look at that angel face.

JOSIE: You see I was looking for someone—its important and I only have two weeks.

BELLE: You can't leave—look how she likes you.

EUGENIA: You'll break her heart—

BELLE: We'll abuse her again.

JOSIE: You abused her?

EUGENIA: We did no such thing. Belle. Don't say that. Don't even joke.

(MR. EVERETT WRIGHT *appears in the doorway. A silhouette.*)

BELLE & JOSIE: Daddy!

(BELLE *runs to his arms.* EVERETT *picks her up and spins her.*)

EVERETT: And who is this?

(JOSIE *stands speechless.*)

EUGENIA: This is our new nanny—we hope—

JOSIE: Josie. Josephine.

EVERETT: Wonderful. I know old Ginnie has needed help. Ever since the baby came she's been clamoring for a nanny—

JOSIE: I—you—

EUGENIA: The girl is freezing you know she walked here all the way from the woods—on a night like this?

EVERETT: Terrible.

BELLE: She has her own car Daddy. I should have my own car.

EVERETT: You should have everything you wish for.

BELLE: Don't forget this time.

EVERETT: I never forget a thing.

EUGENIA: Belle—take her upstairs. Get her some clothes. She can stay in the maid's room behind the kitchen. Mr Livingstone can warm it up for her and make up the bed.

(EUGENIA *and* EVERETT *walk off arm and arm.*)

(JOSIE *stands dumbstruck with the baby in her arms.*)

BELLE: What's wrong with you? You look like you've seen a ghost!

JOSIE: Your father—

BELLE: He's the best. Better than the best. The best father a girl could ever have. Now. Follow me. You can borrow my old nightdress. It should fit.

(BELLE *exits.* JOSIE *doesn't move.*)

BELLE: Come on!

JOSIE: What is his name?

(BELLE *returns, grabs* JOSIE *and pulls her along.*)

BELLE: Everett Wright, my mother's Eugenia Wright and I'm Belle. Belle Wright.

JOSIE: But he's—

BELLE: And you're holding wee Maggie. Maggie Wright. You are a perfect nanny. We're so glad you've come.

(*The lights fade to black.*)

4.

(*Two weeks later*)

(*A soda counter*)

(BELLE *sits with an elaborate pink soda in front of her. Whipped cream. Cherries. Sauce. She drinks with a straw that is bent into a heart.*)

(*She is dressed adorably in layers, boots, stockings, and a sweet, sweet hat.*)

(*The ding of the door*)

(WARREN *enters with an overnight bag. Sits down a stool away from* BELLE.)

(MAN *approaches. Dressed as a soda jerk.*)

MAN: What can I get you young fellow?

WARREN: A coffee.

MAN: Coming right up. Just brewed fresh. You could smell it coming in I bet. Could you smell it coming in? Brings people here for miles the smell of my coffee.

WARREN: Um. Maybe I did? Not consciously.

MAN: Course not consciously. That'd be like advertising and that is not what I do. You're coming from that city over the mountains aren't you?

WARREN: I am. How'd you know?

BELLE: The cut of your jib.

WARREN: My jib?

BELLE: City cut for sure.

WARREN: Hah. Didn't know I was so easy to read.

MAN: You're not. You got off the two o'clock bus.

(Coffee is served.)

WARREN: Right. Thanks. Milk?

MAN: No milk.

BELLE: I'm Belle.

WARREN: Warren.

BELLE: Pleased to meet you Warren. If you don't mind my saying, you look a little lost.

WARREN: Just don't know if I'm in the right place.

BELLE: Always hard to know that isn't it? I never know. But. Here I am. And here you are, so this must be the place to be.

WARREN: I'm looking for someone. I think she came here.

BELLE: Maybe so, we get all sorts coming through. Most don't stay though. It's a little place you know. People don't really want little places to stay in. They just like to visit.

WARREN: It seems like a nice town.

BELLE: Oh yeah. My dad's the mayor.

WARREN: He is?

BELLE: Uh-huh. And my mom's the lady who knows everything.

WARREN: Convenient.

BELLE: Uh-huh. So if you want to know where your girl is you could ask my mom.

WARREN: I didn't say my girl.

BELLE: Oh sorry. Your guy?

WARREN: No. no. A girl. But—I don't know if she is mine. She said she'd call. She said she'd be back in a fortnight. And it's been two weeks and not a word.

BELLE: Maybe something terrible happened to her. An accident? A kidnapping? Maybe she was sold into prostitution by a lascivious gang of n'er do wells.

WARREN: Does that happen out here?

BELLE: Anything can happen anywhere.

WARREN: Oh my god.

BELLE: But no. Not here. My daddy is the chief of police. He'd put a stop to any shenanigans like that.

WARREN: Mayor and police?

BELLE: He's very important.

MAN: Belle—you're expected back at the house.

BELLE: Right. Gotta skidaddle. Warren. I'd like to help you. I'd like to help you find your love.

WARREN: Thanks but—

BELLE: You'll come to dinner. Tonight. You have something nice to wear?

WARREN: I have a clean shirt—

BELLE: That'll do. A car will pick you up out front of here at five. We'll solve all your problems.

WARREN: Thanks. Thanks so much.

(BELLE *takes* WARREN'S *hand with great care.*)

BELLE: Don't mention it. A young man like you should not have to wander long without hope.

She gives him a re-assuring peck on the cheek and exits.

WARREN *stands a bit dumb-struck.*

MAN: If you're done with your coffee. I'm closing up now.

WARREN: Middle of the day?

MAN: Any of your business?

WARREN: Um no. Sorry. Is there a hotel or somewhere I can stay for the night?

MAN: Belle'll help you out. That's a girl you can rely on. That's a girl who calls when she says she will and would never run away on a wild goose chase. That's a girl who can make a man happy.

WARREN: …

MAN: You finished with that?

WARREN: Oh. Yes. Thanks.

MAN: Good right?

WARREN: Delicious. Best coffee I ever had.

MAN: That's what I like to hear.

(WARREN *exits.*)

5.

(*At the house*)

(EVERETT *sits at his desk. He is reading a paper and taking occasional notes.*)

(JOSIE *lurks in the doorway, watching him.*)

(EUGENIA *appears in the doorway, grabs* JOSIE *by the ear and jerks her away.*)

(EVERETT *packs up his papers and exits.*)

(EUGENIA *pulls* JOSIE *onstage by her ear.*)

JOSIE: Ouch! Stop! You're hurting me!

EUGENIA: I see you. I see what you're doing.

JOSIE: I was just watching him.

EUGENIA: Just watching my foot. I see how you look at him. I see how you find a million ways to put yourself beside him. Vying for his attention.

JOSIE: I—it's like he doesn't see me.

EUGENIA: Of course he doesn't see you—you are the help. You are the nanny. He is an upstanding husband. A pillar of the community. A venerable gentleman who does not stoop to wallowing in the muck—

JOSIE: That's not—

EUGENIA: Not what you're doing? You've been here a fortnight and if you were not so good with that baby I would send you packing with no regrets.

JOSIE: Please don't send me away—

EUGENIA: In fact I think you are an impostor.

JOSIE: Wait— Did you say a fortnight?

EUGENIA: The morning after you arrived a rotund woman knocked on the door. In sensible shoes and a smart hat. She said she was the nanny.

JOSIE: It can't have been two weeks.

EUGENIA: And she looked like a nanny but I said, 'you can't be. You came last night. The nanny came last night.' But—she provided a ream of references and I still sent her away.

JOSIE: Mrs Wright—please—how has it been two weeks?

EUGENIA: And I recollected that we were so bowled over by the sudden cessation of that baby's wailing that we never even asked. We never even did a background check.

JOSIE: I need to use the phone—

EUGENIA: But you are a marvel with Mags. An absolute marvel. And in this economy becoming essential to a family of means is really your best bet. But. And I have to underline this, the way you lurk around Mr Wright un-nerves me.

JOSIE: I don't think I'm lurking—

EUGENIA: You suggest something by your very presence.

JOSIE: I'm sure I'm not. I'm not suggesting anything. I'm only interested.

EUGENIA: That's what I'm afraid of—

JOSIE: No—no—not that—I just—if I am going to be an effective nanny for the dear babe then I should know both the parents. I should make a, restrained study of the paternal influence.

EUGENIA: Uh-hmmm

JOSIE: And, this should be done soon don't you think? I should know him well, spend some time. Develop a relationship—

EUGENIA: As you have with me?

JOSIE: As I am attempting with you.

EUGENIA: No more no less.

JOSIE: Nothing more.

EUGENIA: Hmmm. Fine. But. You need a uniform.

JOSIE: Excuse me?

EUGENIA: Your outfits are intrusive.

JOSIE: I don't think my—

EUGENIA: And your hair is distracting. Your hair and your make up. *(She claps twice.)*

(MAN appears with a bundle.)

MAN: You need these?

EUGENIA: Thank you Mr Livingstone. You may give them to Josie.

(MAN does and exits.)

JOSIE: What is— *(She unfolds a long, plain dress of sack cloth. A kerchief for her head. A most un-ironic apron.)*

EUGENIA: An outfit. A regulation, non-provocative, self-eradicating uniform. Put it on.

JOSIE: Now?

EUGENIA: Yes now. You said you needed to know him thoroughly. So—now. Then you can embark on your observations without distraction.

JOSIE: Okay—fine. Do you mind?

(EUGENIA turns to provide privacy. JOSIE changes into the uniform.)

EUGENIA: And all telephone calls are to go through me. You may ask permission and I will grant you a certain number of minutes to speak.

JOSIE: I don't think—

EUGENIA: This is my home. You are in our employ. There are limits to your movements should you wish to stay here. Are you finished?

JOSIE: Finished.

(EUGENIA turns. JOSIE's appearance is quite changed.)

(EUGENIA *circles her like a shark. Adjusting* JOSIE's *hair, her smock.* EUGENIA *spits on her hand and wipes make-up off* JOSIE's *face.*)

EUGENIA: That will do. I will tell Mr Wright to expect you. Collect dear Maggie from her nap. She can accompany you when you interview him. You can witness their interactions and ask whatever questions that you need. Will that suffice?

JOSIE: That would be—that would be perfect.

EUGENIA: Now. I'm off. Belle needs a beau and it's been difficult to locate a suitable suitor in town this time of year.

JOSIE: Could you remind me please—how long have I been here again?

EUGENIA: Two weeks. Are you thick?

JOSIE: No. I guess. I've been so entranced—

EUGENIA: Babies will entrance you.

JOSIE: Those few minutes on the phone. I need them now please. Before Maggie wakes up.

EUGENIA: Fine.

(EUGENIA *claps twice.* MAN *appears with a phone on a silver tray.*)

JOSIE: Thank you.

(EUGENIA *exits.*)

(JOSIE *grabs the phone.*)

JOSIE: Could I have—some privacy?

MAN: Of course. If I may suggest something—

JOSIE: What?

MAN: You may want to use my phone instead.

(MAN *offers her his cell phone.*)

JOSIE: I'm sure this is fine.

MAN: As you will.

(JOSIE *dials, speaks intently but quietly so as not to be overheard.*)

JOSIE: Hello? Hello—Warren? Warren the line is very fuzzy—Warren. I've found him. I've found him— Do you hear me? Warren? Warren?

(*The line is dead.*)

JOSIE: Mr Livingstone?

MAN: Yes.

JOSIE: Could I use your phone?

(BELLE *enters.*)

MAN: I'm sure I don't know what you mean. (*He exits with the phone on the silver tray.*)

BELLE: Oh Josie you've no idea the day I've had! I went to town. There's a sweet town nearby. You should go— once you get settled. And, why are you wearing that?

JOSIE: Your mother—

BELLE: Looks terrible. I was just sitting drinking a cherry cream at the soda counter when the most striking young man walked in. A stranger. And I smiled at him and he smiled back. He was looking for someone. I said who? And he said his one true love. So sweet. He has the best eyes. Like chocolate drops framed by angel wings. And I had some kind of wave of inspiration inspired I'm sure by those eyes of melty goo and I said, you've found her. And he sat down right next to me and we talked and talked and he's coming to dinner tonight. You should hide under the table just to get a look at him you will swoon. You will absolutely swoon. If you like boys. Do you like boys?

JOSIE: Yes—I'm engaged to one.

BELLE: You are? Where's the ring?

JOSIE: He's getting it.

BELLE: Not an engagement until there is a ring.

(A terrible scream erupts from the little door.)

BELLE: Sounds like ol' gassy ass is up. Better hop too!

(JOSIE looks towards the door.)

JOSIE: Belle—actually my fiancé is expecting me to call—I said I'd call every night and I don't know what happened but time passed and now it's so late. He must be so worried and your mother gave me a phone—

BELLE: Oh her phone never works.

JOSIE: Could I use yours? Do you think?

BELLE: Of course! But that baby—

JOSIE: Right. Right. Thank you. Thank you!

(JOSIE disappears into the little door and calms the screaming.)

EVERETT *enters.*

BELLE: Daddy!

(BELLE throws herself into his arms.)

EVERETT: My dearest darling!

BELLE: Daddy we're going to have a guest for dinner.

EVERETT: Mmm. Delicious. I love guest. Roasted I hope.

BELLE: Daddy!

EVERETT: Who will be joining our little band?

BELLE: A dear young man I met in town.

EVERETT: Picking up strays darling Belle?

BELLE: He was so sad. Looking for his love who's gone away.

EVERETT: Poor lad.

BELLE: I cheered him up.

EVERETT: Your sweet face would cheer the saddest heart.

BELLE: Oh daddy.

(JOSIE *is in the doorway holding the baby. Listening*)

EVERETT: It's true sweetheart. Now. I need to get through some of this paperwork before the dinner hour.

BELLE: Yes daddy. Don't work too hard.

EVERETT: I never do.

(BELLE *exits.*)

(JOSIE *enters with the baby.*)

JOSIE: Um—excuse me—

EVERETT: Oh hello Josie. Everything ship shape?

JOSIE: Everything's fine. I just—wanted to talk with you a moment?

EVERETT: Ahhh! Talk with this old blunderbuss. Whyever for? Surely you have better things to do than to natter with an old man.

JOSIE: You're hardly old.

EVERETT: Some mornings I feel I've lived two lifetimes.

JOSIE: Two?

EVERETT: Hah! Imagine.

JOSIE: Do you remember the first?

EVERETT: You know. Sometimes I do. I remember a truck. And a pair of boots—it's the strangest thing—but, it passes quick.

JOSIE: No—no memory is tricky sometimes—was there a house?

EVERETT: Maybe. Blue. Small. So much smaller than here—

JOSIE: It was blue. With a little red door.

EVERETT: A red door? Sounds tacky. I hope Little Mags isn't giving you any trouble?

JOSIE: None at all.

EVERETT: Good.

JOSIE: Mr Wright, when did you come here?

EVERETT: Here? When I married Eugenia. It's her family's house. Fine people the Wrights.

JOSIE: You took her name?

EVERETT: Oh yes. All the men do. As you wind your way through the world you'll find many different traditions. You go along with them you never know where you'll end up.

JOSIE: But—before. What was your name before?

EVERETT: Before?

JOSIE: Before you came here?

EVERETT: What an odd question. What an odd girl you are. Eugenia. Isn't she just the oddest girl?

(EUGENIA *appears*.)

EUGENIA: Yes. Yes she is.

EVERETT: Such a curious thing.

EUGENIA: You know where curiosity got the cat.

EVERETT: Wait- I've heard that one—

JOSIE: Killed.

EVERETT: Oh Ginnie! Always bringing threats of death into conversations. Surely there's no need for that. The girl only wants a chat.

EUGENIA: The girl has work to attend to and I don't see how this is helping her to achieve her duties.

EVERETT: Always on task is my Eugenia.

JOSIE: How did you meet?

EVERETT: In town. I was passing through on business—

EUGENIA: I'm sure the girl's not interested in this ancient history—

JOSIE: What kind of business?

EVERETT: This and that. Different than my job now.

JOSIE: Construction?

EUGENIA: Hah! No. Everett has never been a laborer.

JOSIE: But his hands—

(EVERETT *looks at his hands.*)

EVERETT: I have calluses.

(JOSIE *points to his palms*)

JOSIE: Just like my dad's—there. Where you hold a hammer. There where you hold a saw.

(EUGENIA *steps between* EVERETT *and* JOSIE.)

EUGENIA: Let go of his hands—

EVERETT: Your dad—

JOSIE: He worked construction—he traveled from job to job—when I was twelve he just didn't come back.

EUGENIA: That's quite enough.

EVERETT: How could he leave his daughter?

EUGENIA: Everett. Would you check on Belle? She's flushed beyond reason about this boy who's coming for dinner.

EVERETT: Of course. Josie—

JOSIE: Yes?

EVERETT: You're a great addition to our staff. Don't you agree Ginny?

EUGENIA: Yes. Yes. Indispensable.

(EVERETT *exits.*)

(EUGENIA *whirls around to* JOSIE.)

(EUGENIA *faces her with a face of fire.*)

(*Then breaks down into tears.*)

(JOSIE *is not sure what to do.*)

JOSIE: Mrs. Wright?

EUGENIA: I'm sorry. I'm so sorry.

JOSIE: You stole him. You stole him from me—

EUGENIA: *(Weeping)* No. No—You don't understand. I knew this day would come. I'd hoped it never would—

JOSIE: What day?

EUGENIA: The day a girl would come and turn my happy home upside down.

JOSIE: He's my father—I think he's my father—

(EUGENIA *slaps* JOSIE.)

EUGENIA: Never say that again.

JOSIE: He is! He remembers the house! His hands! He's my father!

(EUGENIA *slaps* JOSIE *again.*)

(JOSIE *stumbles to not drop the baby.*)

EUGENIA: Give me that baby.

(EUGENIA *takes* MAGS *from* JOSIE *as* JOSIE *recovers from the blow.*)

(MAGS *begins to wail.*)

EUGENIA: Shh, shhh. What am I supposed to do? He loves me. He is my family. He is my husband. Don't

you respect that? Don't you see you can't just come in
here and wreck our life? Maggie—shh, shhh—

(JOSIE *holds out her hands.*)

JOSIE: Let me.

(MAGS *is comforted by* JOSIE.)

EUGENIA: What do you think it's like? I can't comfort
my own child. I can't bring her peace—you can.
Imagine. Your daughter preferring a stranger to you.
Imagine your baby screaming at your touch.

JOSIE: I'm sure she'll grow out of it—

EUGENIA: Belle thinks you're fantastic. Bubbles over
to tell you things. Everett looks at you as if you might
hold his heart. Mags—well. You hear her when you're
not around. And I—

JOSIE: What?

EUGENIA: I can see that you're a lovely young woman.
You're competent, you're reasonable, you've grace and
style.

JOSIE: Oh Mrs Wright.

EUGENIA: What do I have? What can my house offer?
He'll leave. He'll leave the moment he remembers. And
then—then what about me? What about Belle? What
about little baby Mags?

JOSIE: I don't want to take him away I just—

EUGENIA: He'll go though. He'll never understand
what brought him here, what kept him here. He's a
good man. Through and through. How do you think
he would feel if you told him that he abandoned his
wife and child? That he simply disappeared from their
lives without a word?

JOSIE: I don't know—

EUGENIA: It would destroy him. Do you want to destroy him?

JOSIE: No—I just wanted to see him. To find him—to let him know I was fine. That I grew up fine. That I'm going to be married to a wonderful man who loves me and I wanted him to walk me down the aisle.

EUGENIA: Of course that's what you want. But you understand. I can't allow you to stay here. I can't allow you to wreck my family.

JOSIE: I won't. I won't wreck anything.

EUGENIA: Every time you speak vipers leap from your tongue and poison my happy home.

JOSIE: I'll stop. I won't say a word.

EUGENIA: You can't promise such a thing. The minute my back is turned you'll start spewing your hopes and dreams all over the place. You'll turn him away from us all. You'll leave Mags a fatherless weeping orphan—

JOSIE: I promise. I won't speak. Just—just let me stay—I want to be near him. I just, I want to be close, to feel close to him again.

EUGENIA: I need an assurance.

JOSIE: Anything.

EUGENIA: I need your tongue.

JOSIE: My—

EUGENIA: You said anything. I don't want to deny you the feeling of a father's love. I don't want to deprive you of your birthright.

JOSIE: But my—

EUGENIA: These are my terms.

JOSIE: I can't—

EUGENIA: You won't feel a thing. I am an expert.

JOSIE: But my voice—

EUGENIA: You wish to know him? You wish to spend time with him? You want him to love you in his way?

JOSIE: I just want to stay.

(EUGENIA *claps twice.* MAN *appears.*)

EUGENIA: Exactly. Mr Livingstone. Ms. Josie would like to stay. She's accepted my terms.

(EUGENIA *slips* MAGS *out of* JOSIE's *arms.* MAGS *wails.*)

MAN: Of course madam.

(MAN *grabs* JOSIE *by the arms.* EUGENIA *pulls out a very long, very sharp knife.* MAGS *in one arm. The knife in the other she approaches* JOSIE.)

(JOSIE *regrets her decision, struggles in vain to escape.*)

EUGENIA: Dear. You must hold still. I know this is a sacrifice but you love him don't you? You love your father? We all make sacrifices to be close to the ones we love. Don't we Mr Livingstone?

MAN: We do.

JOSIE: Please—Please!

EUGENIA: You can leave. You can leave right now. You will never see him again. Can you live with that?

JOSIE: I want—I want him back.

EUGENIA: Then. We are agreed. Say Ahhhh.

JOSIE: Ahhhhh.

(*Blackout*)

END OF ACT ONE

ACT TWO

1.

(JOSIE *alone.*)

JOSIE: What happens when you lose your voice.
Instead of talking you choke up. Like you're going to
cry. All the time. Just to relieve the pressure of all the
things you cannot say. And you can't even remember
why it is that you cannot say them. You tell yourself
they were stupid anyway. Probably they would have
revealed you as the fool you are.
Unfit for human understanding.
Unfit for human conversation.
Unfit for human anything.
So. Better to be silent. Better to go and stick your
head in an oven. Or in a bowl of water. Breathe in
water instead of air. Or in a pillow. Fill yourself with
something different. `
Gas
Water
Feathers
Anything to fill this awful empty.
Anything.

(BELLE *enters. She carries* MAGS *who is screaming.* BELLE *is
glowing with anticipation.*)

BELLE: Josie! Josie! Hold this wretched baby.

(*Hands* MAGS *to* JOSIE. *The crying ceases.*)

BELLE: You are like magic. What did we ever do without you? Now listen—You'll never guess. You'll never ever guess. In fact don't. Don't guess. Just look! *(She holds out her hand to display a sparkling engagement ring.)*
The moment I saw him I knew. I knew it. He would be my own. My dearest darling. The one who would cradle me to sleep every night. And you know it wasn't easy. You know he loved some girl who left him. Left him? Can you imagine! But. Last night—listen. Listen to what he said, he took my hand—like this.
(She takes JOSIE's hand.)
And then he said, "Belle, I want to marry you. I want to put a ring on your finger and wait for you at the end of an aisle and see you emerge all white dressed and flowered and I want to dance with you while our family and friends watch us and I want to love you for ever and ever until we're old and we bicker and we smell and our apartment deteriorates around us and we fall asleep with a kiss and grow cold in the bed and everyone agrees that we had the best ever love because we died together."
(She falls over in a fit of joy.)
Beautiful. Isn't that just the most beautiful thing anyone has ever said to anyone ever? I mean really? Can you imagine? I said yes. I said yes immediately and he said, 'Promise you'll never leave me." And I said of course I'd never leave him. I have everything I need right here. I have a wonderful family and now I have a dear husband. Why would I ever leave! I will love him and stand by him and bear his children and everything! Everything! Ach! There is so much to do. We're getting married in a fortnight! I need a dress and a cake and flowers and a party and some bridesmaids, and Mother! Mother!
(She exits.)

(JOSIE *stands dumbstruck. Moves to follow* BELLE, *but her feet are like lead.*)

(EVERETT *enters. He wears a tuxedo.*)

EVERETT: Ah! Josie. Perfect. Just the girl I need to see.

(JOSIE *stops and turns to* EVERETT. *Her eyes full of longing.*)

EVERETT: Things are going to fly around here for the next couple of weeks—no time to waste. You'll need to be tricksy on your toes. This will be the most perfect wedding since my own Eugenia walked down the aisle. Now, how do I look? I wore this very model for my own wedding, thought I'd give it another whirl at Belle's—not too tight?

(JOSIE *shakes her head.*)

EVERETT: Heh heh heh, the girls keep me fit. Could you give me a hand with this cuff link? It just won't link the cuff. Here, I'll take Mags.
Boody—boody-boo little one. Boody boody boo!

(JOSIE *passes* MAGS *to* EVERETT *and fixes his cuff links. Her hand passes over the callus on his palm.*)

EVERETT: So strange. I barely feel your hand there. The skin is so tough. I've been thinking about it since you asked me where they are from. It's the strangest thing. I don't have a clue. I looked around for some tools, see what matched up with them—how I could have got them but—nothing. You know we have no tools in this house? Hah! Such a life with the Wrights. Such a perfect life. Boody Boo Little Mags you'll be next—I'll be an old man and you may be walking me down the aisle or pushing me in a chair but I will be there. I will be there little one.

(EVERETT *gives* MAGS *a kiss and hands her back to* JOSIE.)

EVERETT: There now. Don't let them work you too hard Josie. You've lost some color since you arrived. Take some time for yourself, get outside. Enjoy the air. The air here is perfect—they took tests and it's clean as a whistle. *(He exits.)*

(JOSIE can't bear for him to leave. Moves to follow him)

(WARREN enters from the opposite door.)

WARREN: Um—excuse me—I'm so sorry to bother you I hope you can help me—I've lost my bags. I came here with an overnight bag and a little suitcase. I don't know where they've gone. I'm not even wearing my own clothes! I mean. These are much nicer than what I arrived in. Everything really. Everything is much nicer than what I arrived in—but I think there was something important in there—

(JOSIE backs away from WARREN.)

WARREN: That I need. Or I thought I needed. What?

(JOSIE stares at WARREN.)

WARREN: What? Why are you looking at me like that? Don't look at me like that. If you haven't seen the bags that's fine. I'm sure they will turn up. And if they don't I'll be fine. Isn't it funny what we think that we need? It turns out we don't need that much. Not that much at all—

(JOSIE starts walking towards WARREN. He backs away.)

WARREN: What? What are you doing? Stop. Stop okay? I'm sorry I bothered you. I'm sorry I asked. I think—Belle is waiting for me in the garden. In the rose garden. It's her favorite place to sit by the roses, under the willow tree, by the babbling brook under the blue blue sky in the sweet clear air—I should find her. I will find her. *(He exits.)*

(JOSIE follows WARREN to the door.)

(EUGENIA appears, stopping her in her path.)

EUGENIA: Why so glum my dear? I'd say things are going swimmingly. Everett is very fond of you. He said just the other day what a lovely nanny you were. He is worried that you spend too much time in the house. He thinks you should get out more.

(JOSIE *glares at* EUGENIA.)

EUGENIA: What? Don't look at me like that. I was only trying to help. You wanted this. How was I supposed to know your fiancé would turn up and flip over our Belle? I'm no future-predictor type. Oh you dear girl, I know this must be difficult for you—but, you know. The choice is made and the chips fall. We make the bed and lie in it. Dig the hole ourselves and all. He said that he'd asked a girl to marry him—you? I suppose you. And that she left him the very same night, promised to return and never did. Not a call. Not a word. He said he'd been asking her to marry him for years and she always said no. So, I'd say. I'd say you're crying over the milk you spilled yourself. Best to sop it up and get on with things. Right? Pull yourself up by your bootstraps. Buck up. Commit to your choices. Tuck your doubts in your heel. That's something there's not enough of these days. Self-reliance. That old stick-to-it-'ve-ness. That's the only way anyone gets anywhere.

(JOSIE *nods, walks up to* EUGENIA, *puts* MAGS *in her arms and exits.*)

EUGENIA: Josie! Josie—where are you going?

(MAGS *starts to cry, softly at first.*)

EUGENIA: Josie—I can't take her today we're tasting cake! We're auditioning bands! We're choosing paper! Napkin rings! Centerpieces! Doilies! The Doily Lady will be here any minute!

(MAGS *crying grows louder.*)

EUGENIA: There there—Maggie dear. Maggie. Don't cry. Don't—don't shhh. Shhh. Mommy is here. Mommy is here—

(MAGS *screams*.)

EUGENIA: Josie! Josie! Please. Please wait—wait! I can help! I can help you!

(JOSIE *re-enters*.)

EUGENIA: Stubborn girl. See—this is what's wrong with you. You can't commit to a course of action. You must commit to something to get what you want—

(JOSIE *moves to go again*.)

EUGENIA: Fine! Fine! Come back! Take her back, please! Take her back! OUCH! She bit me! The damn baby bit me with her tooth! When did she grow a tooth? Dammit. Take her.

(JOSIE *crosses her arms*.)

EUGENIA: Your face will freeze that way. You know that right? Freeze that way and you'll never get a man.

(*An awful scream*.)

EUGENIA: Ach! Fine. Look. Look. You want your father? You want to know him? Really know him? Fine. Perhaps you can find him—some small sliver of him in the basement. He visits his things there—I'll tell you where. Just take this baby—

(JOSIE *reaches out for* MAGS, EUGENIA *hands her over*.)

EUGENIA: Ach. Babies. Babies are the worst.

(MAGS *quiets in* JOSIE's *arms*.)

EUGENIA: Now. After your visit to Everett's little hidey hole, you need to get Ms. Belle ready for this wedding, hair, nails, make-up, dress her up good and that's not all. She's a bit of a naive self-centered little thing and that can push a man away as much as a sloven

appearance—or running away in the middle of the
night to pursue some long dead dream! At any rate. If
this wedding doesn't come off without a hitch, if my
dearest Belle doesn't keep his heart tied up tight with
hers the gig's up.
(*She leans over* MAGS.
She's such a peach with you. Such a peach I could just
gobble her up. Yummy Yummy Yummy.
How are you at creating cascading curls?

(JOSIE *shakes her head no.*)

EUGENIA: Pity. Well. You'll figure it out. You best or
I'll lock you out back with the pigs and the hedgehogs.
Your dear poppa never goes back there at all.
(*She exits.*)

(JOSIE *alone with* MAGS. JOSIE *follows seeking directions for
the promised basement.*)

(*The* MAN *appears.*)

MAN: You may follow me.

(JOSIE *looks questioningly.*)

MAN: What? To your father. I'll take you.

(JOSIE'*s eyes widen.*)

MAN: If you want to go there. Do you want to go there?

(JOSIE *hesitates.*)

MAN: She doesn't lie. His things are there. He may
remember you for a moment.

(JOSIE *steps closer as if to follow.*)

MAN: If that's what you want—is that what you want?
There's always the door and the road.

(JOSIE *considers this option.*)

MAN: We all give up something to be near the ones we
love. Here. Let me take her a moment.

(MAN *gently takes* MAGS. *She coos and coos.*)

MAN: Small comforts are, after all, comforts.

(JOSIE *exits with the* MAN.)

2.

(*A dimly lit basement. An unused workbench. A trunk. A glow off-stage. A muffled radio playing a baseball game*)

(EVERETT *listens to the game. He wears a pair of boots and a flannel work shirt.*)

(JOSIE *tiptoes towards the light.*)

EVERETT: Who is there? What are you doing here?

(JOSIE *looks at him with longing.*)

EVERETT: Who told you about this place?

(JOSIE *shakes her head.*)

EVERETT: Mr Livingstone? Was it him? This is my only secret and what does he do? Blabs it to the first tom, dick or harry who asks. Well. What do you want?

(JOSIE *tries in vain to speak.*)

EVERETT: Speak up. No need to be shy. I'm sure you didn't just wander down here.

(JOSIE *reaches for* EVERETT'*s flannel shirt.*)

EVERETT: Found it in that old trunk. That and these boots. Fit me perfectly. Didn't even need to wear them in. Strangest thing—I feel sad wearing them. But sad in a good way. You ever feel that?

(JOSIE *throws herself against* EVERETT. *Crying*)

EVERETT: Now now—whoa there—whoa there girl, what's the matter? Stop that now. Stop that—

(EVERETT *pushes* JOSIE *away.*)

EVERETT: There there now—that's no way to behave.
Crying never got anyone anywhere. Come on now.
You got something bothering you what you need to do
is—all you can do is—

(JOSIE *stands staring at* EVERETT.)

EVERETT: All you can do is…
(*He backs up.*)
What you do is…
Well. There. You see. I'm no one to give advice. I'm no
one to talk to about your troubles. See? I don't know
anything about a girl's troubles. I never have been able
to make heads or tails of what any one of them wanted.
I mean. I see you want something. I see you need
something from me. You're expecting something. You
are aren't you? You look at me like—like I can—like I
can solve the world for you.
I can't. Josie. I can't. You understand? I just—can't.
Don't ask me to.
Now, you need to get on back upstairs, I'm sure that
little screamer must be waking by now. She'll miss
you. She'll need you.
Don't look at me like that. Don't. Stop it. Stop it right
now. What do you think is supposed to happen? What
do you think is going to happen? It's not going to be
what you want. It's not. It never will.

(JOSIE *launches herself at* EVERETT. *Pummels him with her
fists.*)

EVERETT: Stop! Stop! Josie! Cut it out.

(EVERETT *tries to restrain* JOSIE.)

EVERETT: Don't do this Josie. Stop! Stop it! I can't help. I
can't! Don't you understand!

(WARREN *enters.*)

WARREN: Mr Wright?

EVERETT: You too? What are you doing here?

WARREN: What did you say to her?

EVERETT: Nothing! I said nothing to her! She's crazy!

(JOSIE *refutes this statement.*)

WARREN: Calm down. Stop okay? Here—here—I have paper—I have a pen—you can—you can write it down. Okay? Okay? (*He offers a scrunched up piece of paper and a pencil nub.*)

(JOSIE *snatches the items and begins to write, covering the page.*)

(EVERETT *puts himself back together.*)

EVERETT: Now you listen to me little girl. I don't know who you think you are but you don't act like that. I don't care what you think someone has done or hasn't done. You don't act like that. No daughter of mine would behave that way. No daughter of mine would ever act like that.

WARREN: She's trying to say something—give her a second.

EVERETT: No. She will gather her things and be out by the end of the day. You understand? I have a family to look after and she is not the sort we want around.

(JOSIE *presses her paper at him.* EVERETT *takes it and glances it over and gives it back to her.*)

EVERETT: Scribblety scratch. This is nothing but scriblety scratch. I'll explain to Eugenia. Mr Livingstone will have your items waiting for you at the door. And any monies owed. Warren? You'll come with me. (*He exits.*)

(WARREN *pauses. Takes the paper from* JOSIE.)

WARREN: He's right you know. This is—this is just curlie-cues and hearts. I—I'm sorry. I'm sorry he fired you.

EVERETT: *(Off-stage)* WARREN! Leave that girl alone!

(WARREN pauses with JOSIE for a moment.)

WARREN: I'm sure you'll find something else soon. *(He turns to exit.)*

(JOSIE tackles WARREN.)

WARREN: Ow! What the—

(JOSIE flips him over and kisses him on the mouth.)

WARREN: Mmm—mmmm

(JOSIE stops and looks at WARREN.)

WARREN: Why are you—

(JOSIE kisses WARREN again. Stops and looks at him)

WARREN: Are you trying to —

(JOSIE kisses WARREN again. This time he kisses back.)

WARREN: I know that mouth—I know that spit—I know you—I know I remember—some other place—an apartment?

(JOSIE nods in agreement.)

WARREN: A dog.

(JOSIE shakes her head no.)

WARREN: A car—you took my car—you were—we were—we were going to get—we were going to get married but you left. You left and you didn't come back—why didn't you come back? I waited and I waited and I went to find you and—you're here. How are you here?

(JOSIE shakes her head.)

WARREN: Because I'm—I'm going to get married. Soon.
To a girl who—

(JOSIE *shakes her head no.*)

WARREN: Tell me. Tell me what's going on. Tell me
what happened to you—to me—where are we? I got
off a bus and Josie—Josie—it was like a fog fell down
over me. A pink and frilly fog—

(JOSIE *tries to act out what happened to her.*)

(WARREN *guesses along.*)

WARREN: You were driving—you stopped for gas—
no—the woods? Yes—there was a storm—oh. Terrible
you should have called triple A—oh. Right. We should
have had that. You went up the hill—uh-huh. There
was a duck?—a monster? No. A Baby? Mags? Mags!
Right—and—then you—

(JOSIE *freezes.*)

WARREN: What? And then what happened?

(EUGENIA *is at the door.*)

EUGENIA: And then nothing happened. Right dear?
Warren—Belle is waiting for you—she wishes you
would visit with her. She wishes it so much. I think it's
the only thing that would make her happy and I want
her to be happy.

WARREN: Mrs Wright. The craziest thing has
happened—this is Josie.

EUGENIA: I know who she is.

WARREN: No. But not just a Josie. My Josie—she's my
fiancé. Was my fiancé.

EUGENIA: She was?

WARREN: She had to find her father but something
happened—

EUGENIA: Oh no. What happened dear?

(JOSIE *stands mute.*)

WARREN: Was there an accident?

EUGENIA: Did you fall on something?

WARREN: Did you get sick?

EUGENIA: Did you find yourself wanting something that this man could never give you?

WARREN: Did you forget about me?

EUGENIA: Oh Warren. I think she forgot about you. I think that. What she can't say is that. Once she left you seemed very far away like you had never existed in the first place.

WARREN: Josie?

(JOSIE *glares at* EUGENIA.)

EUGENIA: I'm so sorry Warren. Sometimes it's difficult to put painful truths into words.

WARREN: But—

EUGENIA: Go on now. Belle is waiting. Don't worry—this will—this will fade.

WARREN: Josie? Is this true?

(JOSIE *looks at* WARREN, *shakes her head.*)

EUGENIA: She's so sorry Warren. So sorry. She's so glad Belle is there for you. Waiting for you.

WARREN: Belle is—

EUGENIA: Waiting for you. Go on. She made cupcakes I think. Butter cream frosting. Champagne.

WARREN: I love cupcakes.

EUGENIA: I know dear. Go on now.

WARREN: (*To* JOSIE) Would you like to come?

EUGENIA: Oh no. She's very busy. You go ahead. I'll be up in a minute.

WARREN: Okay. Thanks. Thank you Mrs Wright. *(He exits.)*

EUGENIA: Well now. Josie Josie Josie. You think Warren just needs to remember you? You think Everett just needs to recall his young fatherhood and poof all will be as it was? You actually think that you are that special? Dear. I'm sorry. But. There is nothing special about you. Nothing about you that will cause the ones you love to love you back. They are both happy here. They are cared for here. What can you give them? You weren't even happy when you had them. Remember? Restless. You were no home for them. Don't you want them to be happy? Don't you want them to have a home?

Mr Livingstone!

(MAN enters with MAGS in a perambulator trailing lace, flowers and satin ribbons.)

MAN: I'm sorry m'am. There was some difficulty with the procurement of lace and the bridesmaid's dresses are turning out more like sacks than vases.

EUGENIA: Fine fine fine. Mags is staying with Josie. You need anything for the baby Mr Livingstone will bring it.

MAN: Of course.

(JOSIE shakes her head, pushes the baby carriage away.)

EUGENIA: Uh-uh-uh—you took on a responsibility when you entered our house and a responsibility is not something you can shirk. You're lucky I don't lock you up in the hen yard you little beast. And if you interfere one whit with this wedding I will without waiting. Do not test me.

(EUGENIA exits with the MAN.)

(JOSIE is left with the baby.)

(MAGS *screams.*)

(*Lights shift.*)

JOSIE: What happens when you lose your voice.
You crawl somewhere far inside yourself.
You get lost in caverns of forgotten time.
You stumble onto memories better left untouched.
You imagine that you've said what you've meant even though you never did.
You remember that even when you had your tongue, you didn't say what you meant to say.
A lot of times you said the opposite.
And that didn't help anyone.
But you would have said.
I love you.
I need you.
I think of you and when I think of you instead of you there's a horrible hole in me. A hole like a forest where nothing is as it seems and nobody knows who I am and its so dark and topsy turvy that I got lost before I even started and I need your light to lead me out again.

(*Light shifts.*)

(JOSIE *checks* MAGS. *She's wet and whimpering.*)

(JOSIE *goes to search for a diaper in the carriage.*)

(*Pulls out tulle. Pulls out lace. Pulls out a wedding dress.*)

(*Pulls out a diaper.*)

(*Blackout*)

3.

(EVERETT *paces discontentedly.*)

(BELLE *runs past weeping.*)

BELLE: You're horrible! Horrible! You don't love me! And I'm the most beautiful!

(WARREN *follows at* BELLE's *heels.*)

WARREN: I'm sorry—I do—it's just—

BELLE: Did you even like my cupcakes?

WARREN: Yes?

BELLE: No you didn't. You didn't even have seconds.

(BELLE *storms off.* WARREN *is out of breath with the chase.*)

WARREN: Josie—I mean—Belle—don't go! Dammit. Where's my head?

EVERETT *watches curiously.*

EVERETT: What did you say to her?

WARREN: Nothing—nothing.

EVERETT: That'll do it. You've got to say something. Preferably the right thing at the right time. You'll need some practice. It'll come.

WARREN: I said I was an architect.

EVERETT: You didn't follow me.

WARREN: Excuse me?

EVERETT: Before. I said to leave that girl alone and you didn't.

WARREN: Oh. Right.

EVERETT: I said she was fired and now she's got Mags and she's in my special spot.

WARREN: Um.

EVERETT: That was my spot. I didn't give it to her.

What did you want to build?

WARREN: What?

EVERETT: Said you were an architect. What did you want to build?

WARREN: Oh—um. Houses? Homes for people.

EVERETT: You could do that?

WARREN: I can draw up plans. Estimate materials. Find a contractor.

EVERETT: You're not totally useless.

WARREN: Um. No. Not useless.

EVERETT: Must feel good.

WARREN: Excuse me?

EVERETT: To have a skill.

WARREN: I need to make a living.

EVERETT: Not any more. Now everything's taken care of.

WARREN: I can take care of myself though, I mean I appreciate the generosity, but I can't just not do anything.

EVERETT: You'll be Belle's husband. Isn't that enough?

WARREN: I don't know—are you happy here?

EVERETT: I have never known a moment of sorrow.

WARREN: I wondered with your um, your workshop—

EVERETT: That nanny's in there now. I didn't tell her she could stay.

WARREN: She was very upset.

EVERETT: I don't want her there. I don't want her near me.

WARREN: She was upset with you—she thinks she knows you.

EVERETT: No. She's just a lost girl who thinks that someone can save her. Well. No one here can do that so the quicker she hits the road the better.

WARREN: What do you think she wants?

EVERETT: How in blazes am I supposed to know? I never did know—how am I supposed to know now?

WARREN: We could ask her—I—I would like to ask her.

EVERETT: No. No. No. We've got the cigars and the whiskey. The wisdom to impart and a wedding to prepare for.

WARREN: Just—maybe we should talk to her again. She was so upset before—

EVERETT: No no no, you start worrying about one sad one and you'll never be done with it. Now, I've got a whiskey that you won't believe—

(EVERETT *shuffles* WARREN *away from the door.*)

4.

(JOSIE *stares at a wedding dress.*)

(MAGS *starts to cry from the pram.* JOSIE *goes to hold her.*)

(BELLE *sneaks up to the door. Peeks in*)

(JOSIE *adjusts the dress.*)

BELLE: Oh wow!

(JOSIE *startles.*)

BELLE: Sorry—sorry—I didn't mean to startle you—is that—is that a wedding dress?

(JOSIE *nods.*)

(JOSIE *settles* MAGS *in the pram.*)

BELLE: It's beautiful. It's so much better than the one
Mr Livingstone made for me. That one's like a Ferrari
smashed through a down comforter—but this one—
(She regards the dress.)
Oh Josie! Josie! Tell me I can wear it? Tell me it's for
me. It's for me right?

(JOSIE hesitates.)

BELLE: A good dress is the petal and the girl's the
bloom—the scent—the oomph in the middle that
draws the bees.
(She takes the dress.)
This is a good dress.
(She holds it up to herself. Admiringly)
Yes yes yes. Oh Josie. He's losing interest. Already. It's
only been a fortnight—

(JOSIE's eyebrows raise.)

BELLE: I know—it feels like years! But only two weeks
and I've been so busy with the planning—the morels to
go with the lamb the string quartet that evolves into a
brass combo for the dancing, and the decorations—I'm
doing all doilies and flowers. Everything will be petals
and lace—can you imagine? Maybe I've neglected him.
He's, he's thinking of his old life. He suggested that we
live in some tiny apartment in the city? He wants to
be an architect? It's like he doesn't remember that he's
happy here. That everything that he ever needs is right
here.
Is that the veil?
(She tries on the veil.)
Why would he want anything else? Why? Aren't I
pretty enough? Aren't I? Momma says I'm the most
beautiful. Daddy too—but maybe they're lying. Maybe
everyone's just lying and really I'm the most horrible.
Tell me. Tell me for true Josie. Am I horrible?

(JOSIE *pauses.*)

(MAN *enters.*)

MAN: Belle. Your mother expects you posthaste. The champagne and oyster brunch with your aunts is commencing imminently.

BELLE: Argh! Always with the champagne and the oysters. Fine. I'll be right there. So sad you can't join us—momma said no though. She said you had to mind little Mags.

(JOSIE *nods.*)

BELLE: Now, Josie—I want this dress

(MAN *lingers.*)

MAN: It's a lovely dress.

BELLE: Isn't it?

MAN: Too bad it won't be perfect.

BELLE: It's better than the one you made.

MAN: It is. Much better. But still -

BELLE: But it has to be! It must make everyone love me and cut off their arms to protect me!

MAN: That would be quite a dress. But. It will have to be tailored especially for you and that takes time. Your mother won't like it.

BELLE: I don't care what mother wants. This is my wedding.

(JOSIE *stares at the* MAN.)

MAN: You should stay here then. Let Josie do it.

(JOSIE *raises her eyebrows.*)

MAN: Josie can make it fit just right. Hold you tight in all the right places—

BELLE: She can?

MAN: I think she can do whatever she sets her mind to.

(JOSIE *nods slowly.*)

BELLE: Go Mr Livingstone, tell Momma not to worry.

MAN: Of course. Take your time. I'll make certain she doesn't disturb you.
Shall I take Mags for you Ms Josie?

(JOSIE *questions this.*)

MAN: It's not a problem. She is quite fond of me.

(JOSIE *nods.*)

(MAN *exits with* MAGS.)

(JOSIE *takes the dress from* BELLE.)

BELLE: Oh Josie. I am so lucky. Do you know? Do you know how lucky I am? The world just spins and brings me exactly what I wish for. Daddy says its because I'm just so sweet. I think it's the world's way of saying thank you for being such a dear hearted girl. You must have just done something awful to be stuck here without your voice. Momma says that everyone gets exactly what they deserve. What did you do? Were you mean to something soft and furry? Were you ungrateful? You seem so nice but really, you wouldn't be stuck being a nanny if you hadn't of done something wrong along the line. Was it something dirty? Drugs? Sex? Dirty sexy drugs?

(JOSIE *pauses.*)

BELLE: It was wasn't it? I could tell. You have that hollow look about you. Like you'll always be searching for something that you can never find.

(JOSIE *puts the dress in front of herself and looks in the mirror.*)

BELLE: Oh. Poor Josie. Look at you. Some girls just aren't made for happiness.

But you make the best of it. The best of what you have. *(She begins to undress.)*

(Lights fade out.)

5.

(The wedding)

(There is music wafting in. There is a trellis adorned with flowers for the couple to be wed under.)

(EUGENIA stands with EVERETT overseeing the expanse of wedding.)

EUGENIA: She won't see me. Mr Livingstone says she won't see me. Her own mother.

EVERETT: I'm sure she's fine.

EUGENIA: She'll make a mess of it.

EVERETT: She's grown. Don't worry.

EUGENIA: I'm not worried. I just don't want her walking out here looking foolish.

EVERETT: I know dear.

EUGENIA: I want this to be absolutely perfect.

EVERETT: It will be.

EUGENIA: She was uncertain before. Doubts and questions.

EVERETT: You know what you say about doubts and questions.

EUGENIA: Stick them in your heel. But—

EVERETT: What dearest?

EUGENIA: But we have them.

EVERETT: You?

EUGENIA: Of course I do. Of course. I am no monster. It takes a firm mind to push doubt down. It takes a humble heart to acknowledge there are rules that are not to be questioned.

EVERETT: My questions and my doubts were lost years ago.

EUGENIA: You were not happy when you came.

EVERETT: No?

EUGENIA: You were lost. You had a wolf behind your eye. You were dislocated and restless.

EVERETT: You erased that.

EUGENIA: You were relieved.

EVERETT: I became yours. But I lost something.

EUGENIA: Shhhh, let it go. Enjoy the wedding—it's just what you imagined.

(WARREN *enters dressed as a groom.*)

EVERETT: Warren my boy! There you are ready to walk down that aisle. Ready to become a lawful wedded Wright.

(EVERETT *straightens* WARREN's *tie, pats him on the back.*)

WARREN: Well thanks. My stomach is dropping. My mouth is dry. My eyes won't focus right.

EUGENIA: That's normal.

WARREN: It's like I'm shedding something.

EVERETT: You are my boy! You are.

EUGENIA: I should check on her.

EVERETT: She's fine.

WARREN: Belle?

EUGENIA: Wouldn't let me see her.

EVERETT: She's grown.

EUGENIA: I should go.

EVERETT: Eugenia—

EUGENIA: I know I know I know—I'm just going to go have a peek.

(MAN *enters blocking her path.* MAN *has* MAGS *strapped to his chest in a baby carrier.*)

MAN: Ms Belle has sent me to let you know that she is prepared and she will begin when the opening chords of the infamous song reach her ears.

EUGENIA: I'll just check and make sure she's—

MAN: Ms Belle is radiant. She's excited to begin. And. The guests are waiting.

EUGENIA: But—

EVERETT: Well. Let's get this show on the road then. Warren—escort Mrs Wright. Mr Livingstone, cue the music.

(MAN *does. Music begins.*)

(WARREN *proffers his arm to* EUGENIA *who takes it, he leads her to her place beside the trellis.* WARREN *stands waiting.*)

(*The bride emerges and goes to* EVERETT. *She is completely veiled.*)

(EVERETT *holds his arm out and a hand emerges from the pile of tulle to take it, to clutch it, to lean into it.*)

(*They walk down the aisle.*)

(MAN, MAGS *on his chest, takes his post in front of the trellis. Ready to serve as pastor.*)

(EUGENIA *stands up and gapes—along with everyone else at the sight of the dress.*)

(EVERETT *proudly walks his daughter down the aisle.*)

(The beautiful white dress follows next to him, EVERETT
delivers her to WARREN. *Shaking his hand and withdrawing*
to be next to EUGENIA.*)*

MAN: Welcome. The Wright family thanks you all for
being here today. For traveling from locations far and
wide to witness this marriage, these two young people
stepping into the roles that will buttress us all against
the ravages of inconstant time.

(He opens a formidable book and reads.)

Marriage is the moment of happily ever after. It is the
departure from the nest of childhood to the home of
adulthood. By embarking on this commitment a leap of
faith is taken that continues air born until death brings
the ground slamming into your faces faster than any of
you can imagine.

Young Woman, are you prepared to have and to hold
to cling and to absorb to give everything and take
nothing from your groom in sickness and in health till
death do you part?

*(*BELLE *appears, disheveled and trailing tulle and ribbons*
behind her.)

BELLE: STOP! Stop it!

EUGENIA: Belle!

WARREN: Belle?!

EVERETT: What the devil is going on?

MAN: *(To* JOSIE*)* Say it. You must say it!

*(*JOSIE *shakes her head. Her voice isn't back.)*

BELLE: THAT is not me in that dress. That is the maid!
The nanny! She tricked me! She strapped me down
with ribbons and lace! I've been gnawing through the
garlands for the past hour and a half and I see that I've
arrived just in time—

(BELLE *pulls the veil off of* JOSIE *and pulls* WARREN *to her side.* MAGS *starts screamy-crying.*)

BELLE: You were right mother—she is an awful, jealous thing. She wants everything that is mine. What's wrong with you? Don't you have anything of your own?

(JOSIE *still cannot speak.*)

EUGENIA: Would someone please quiet that baby down?

(MAN *hands* MAGS *to* JOSIE. *When he does,* JOSIE *starts to scream as* MAGS *quiets down.* JOSIE *is just as surprised as everyone else.*)

JOSIE: Wahhhhhh-AHHHHHH

WARREN: What's wrong? What's wrong with her?

(*Everyone backs away from* JOSIE, *leaving her alone with* MAGS, *screaming.*)

BELLE: She's worse than that baby—

EVERETT: Josie? Josie? Stop—stop screaming—

EUGENIA: Take that child away from her!

JOSIE: This is my father! This is my Warren! Warren—remember? Remember me? Josie? We live in an apartment by an expressway? Sometimes it seems like it's poisoned? But we won't be there forever. You wanted to marry me but I kept saying not yet not yet but not because I didn't love you—I loved you—I love you—but I thought I was missing something I thought I was missing my father—But now I've found him and it's him but it's not him and he doesn't even know who I am—I don't know—I don't know if he'll ever remember me.

(JOSIE *turns to look at* EVERETT.)

JOSIE: He looks through me. I don't look like I used to—I'm taller. I'm changed. I'm grown and he doesn't even know me. How could he? I'm not the kid he left. I'm a stranger standing here. And you left. You left me. Never even looked back—

EVERETT: I didn't want to go—

JOSIE: But you did. You did go—

EVERETT: Remember Josie? Don't you remember?

JOSIE: You were gone.

EVERETT: I was sick. My body was leaving you—I didn't want to go—

JOSIE: But you did—

EVERETT: I didn't have a choice.

JOSIE: But you're here. You're happy.

EVERETT: No. I'm just—here.

JOSIE: But—

EVERETT: Until you say good -bye—

JOSIE: But I only just found you—

EVERETT: So now you can.

(EVERETT *is weakening.* EUGENIA *goes to him. Supports him.*)

EUGENIA: You couldn't leave him alone could you? He could have stayed here just fine with us, forever happy—forever perfect—

JOSIE: Stop it! Shut up! What's wrong with him?

(EVERETT *is growing weaker and weaker.*)

EUGENIA: He's dying. Because you just couldn't play along?

JOSIE: No—

EUGENIA: He's not lost, he doesn't have to die. Just be quiet and let him forget you again. Come on Belle—get that dress off of her. Warren you stay right there. Let me fix this debacle.

EVERETT: Josie.

JOSIE: Daddy—

EVERETT: Let me go—

JOSIE: I don't want you to die.

EVERETT: You can't stop that. You never could.

JOSIE: All I know is missing you.

EVERETT: Just say good-bye. Josie. You're grown. You can now—

EUGENIA: Obviously she doesn't want to. Obviously she wants to linger here and suffer. Obviously she's not ready to deal with anything more—that's fine. We'll make a place for you in the basement dear. Your father will live happily ever after and you can watch. You can make that happen. Don't you want that?

JOSIE: Yes. I want that.

EVERETT: No.

JOSIE: But we could be together—

EVERETT: Josie, no.

EUGENIA: If you say it, it is just an ending. Not a happy one.

EVERETT: You remember.

JOSIE: You were upstairs. I couldn't go in the room. I couldn't let you go—

EVERETT: You can do it now.

JOSIE: I don't want to.

EVERETT: Think of yourself. Think of Warren. Think of what you'll do—what you'll make—who you'll make—

JOSIE: I only think of you. Of you behind the door and I peek in and you don't have words anymore. You have a rattle in your heart and you look at me and you want me to have everything but I look back and everything is disappearing.

EVERETT: Poor little Jay-bird don't you see what's around you?

JOSIE: I see you.

EVERETT: Close your eyes. See something else.

JOSIE: I can't.

EVERETT: Try.

JOSIE: What will happen?

EVERETT: I don't know.

JOSIE: I love you.

EVERETT: I love you too Jay-bird.

JOSIE: Good-bye.

EVERETT: There you go.

EUGENIA: No! No! Stop it now!

JOSIE: Goodbye Daddy.

(JOSIE *gives* EVERETT *a kiss goodbye.*)

BELLE: Mommy! Mommy? What's happening? Mommy!

EUGENIA: Stop this! Stop this right now!

JOSIE: Goodbye Eugenia, goodbye pretty Belle— Goodbye Mr Livingstone. And Maggie—Little Maggie—Mag-pie—

(Lights come up so bright and then—poof! An explosion of feathers.)

(There is only JOSIE *and* WARREN *left.)*

*(*JOSIE *has her eyes closed tight. Slowly opens them.)*

JOSIE: Warren?

WARREN: Yes?

JOSIE: You've got your fingers and toes?

WARREN: Um—yes. I do. You?

JOSIE: Accounted for.

WARREN: What happened?

JOSIE: A heart-clearing.

WARREN: It's done?

JOSIE: I think—I think we can go home now.

WARREN: It might be poisoned.

JOSIE: No. No. It's a sweet apartment.

WARREN: It is.

JOSIE: Unless we have a baby—it's not a good apartment for a baby.

WARREN: We're going to have a baby?

JOSIE: Maybe.

WARREN: You'll marry me?

JOSIE: Yes.

WARREN: Good. This time I am ready. G P S chip and everything.

JOSIE: So am I. Ready. *(She faces him.)*

*(*JOSIE *and* WARREN *kiss.)*

(The lights fade out leaving them in silhouette.)

END OF PLAY